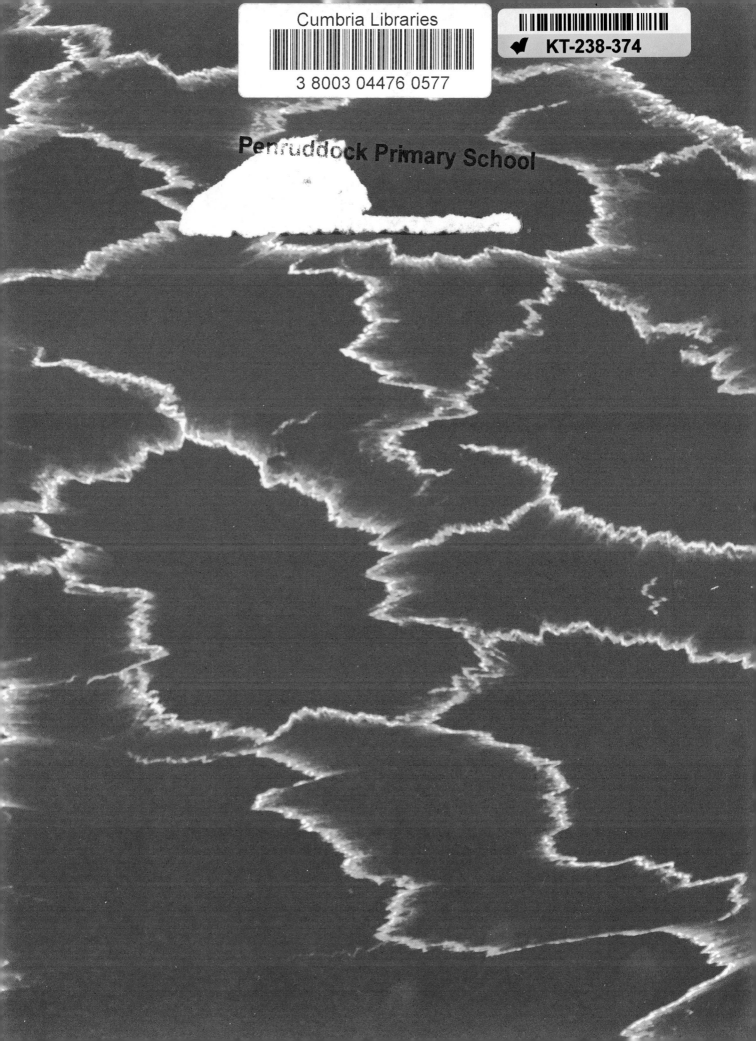

MY TOURIST GUIDE TO
THE CENTRE OF THE EARTH

LONDON, NEW YORK, MELBOURNE,
MUNICH, AND DELHI

Written and edited by Lizzie Munsey

Designer Fiona Macdonald
Additional designer Daniela Boraschi
Senior editor Ben Morgan
Illustrators Katie Knutton, Maltings Partnership,
Peter Bull Art Studio
Producer, pre-production Lucy Sims
Senior producer Alice Sykes
Senior jacket designer Mark Cavanagh
Jacket editor Manisha Majithia
Design development manager Sophia Tampakopoulos
Managing editor Julie Ferris
Managing art editor Owen Peyton Jones
Publisher Sarah Larter
Associate publishing director Liz Wheeler
Art director Phil Ormerod
Publishing director Jonathan Metcalf

Consultant Dr David Rothery, Open University

First published in Great Britain in 2013 by
Dorling Kindersley Limited
80 Strand, London WC2R 0RL
A Penguin Company

Copyright © 2013 Dorling Kindersley Limited
2 4 6 8 10 9 7 5 3 1
001-187010-May/2013

A CIP catalogue record for this book
is available from the British Library

ISBN 978-1-4093-2443-0

Printed and bound in China by Hung Hing

Discover more at
www.dk.com

CONTENTS

PREPARING FOR
YOUR TRIP

You're about to go on an incredible journey – a trip through the Earth, starting above the atmosphere and ending up inside the core. Your ship is essential to your survival in this hostile and turbulent environment – it is carefully designed to take you safely through your journey. Familiarize yourself with it now so that you can make the most of your trip.

Solar panels
These panels let you use the power of the Sun to charge your craft before you head inside Earth.

Living quarters
The residential and research area rotates to stay upright, so you're always the right way up, whatever the ship is doing.

Equipment room
All the clothes and tools you'll need for your adventure can be found in this room.

Cloud vacuum
This device sucks in clouds and feeds them through to the cloud condenser to make water. Make sure you stock up on clouds as you descend through the atmosphere.

Oxygen supplies
There won't always be enough air inside Earth – these backup tanks make sure you won't run out.

Drill
Much of Earth is solid rock – you'll need to drill your way through it.

Controls
Your ship is a complex machine. These instruments allow it to be piloted very precisely.

Helicopter blades
You'll need flying power to get through the atmosphere.

Geothermal engine
These engines will let you power the ship using the heat of the Earth.

Propellers
Your ship needs to be able to travel through liquid as well as air and rock.

Cockpit
This is where everything on board is controlled and monitored.

Seismic sonar unit
Sonar lets you plan your route, so you can find your way even when you can't see where you're going.

Refrigeration system
An advanced cooling system will stop your ship from melting, even at extreme temperatures.

On-board laboratory
Do some research here, or take a closer look at specimens you collect on your trip.

Living accommodation
The crew and passengers sleep in bunk beds to save space.

Cloud condenser
This device takes clouds that have been sucked in by the vacuum and converts them into drinking water for your trip.

ATMOSPHERE

CRUST

MANTLE

CORE

SEE THE EARTH FROM SPACE

To fully appreciate the beauty of our home planet, enjoy a view of it from outer space. This layered ball of rock is thought to have formed about 4.5 billion years ago. Clouds of dust particles around the Sun grew larger and then crashed into each other, eventually coming together to form Earth. The planet looks a bit like a blue marble from space, with bands of clouds swirling over ocean water, land masses, and ice caps at the North and South Poles.

Cloud
Earth has a unique and diverse weather system.

THE MOON

The Moon orbits the Earth once every 27.3 days, and we always see the same side of it from Earth. The continuous pull of gravity between the Earth and the Moon creates the tides of Earth's oceans. Take a Moon orbit tour to photograph the Moon from all angles.

WEATHER

Earth has a wide range of weather, from glorious sunshine to light drizzle to heavy downpours, snow, and thunderstorms. You'll need suncream as well as an umbrella.

Land
Earth's land supports a
wide range of habitats,
from deserts to rainforests.

Earth exploration

"Lots of life"
"The Brazilian rainforest safari was
great, there were hundreds of
different types of animals living
in just one tree."

⭐⭐⭐⭐☆

Activity: rainforest exploration

"Boring!"
"Ice cap skiing sounds like fun,
but we skied for hours and all
we could see was more and
more snow."

⭐☆☆☆☆

Activity: ice cap skiing

ATMOSPHERE

CRUST

MANTLE

CORE

Watery planet
You won't find this much
water anywhere else in
the Solar System!

Three quarters
of the **Earth's**
surface is covered
with **water.**

Polar ice cap
The Earth's South Pole
is capped with solid ice.

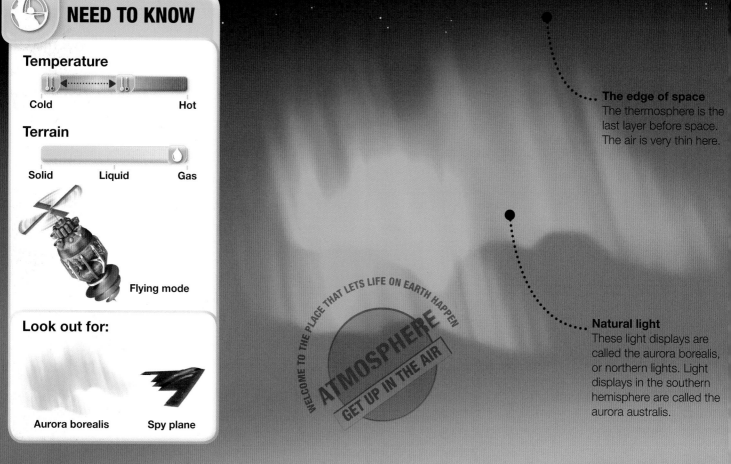

Temperature

Cold   Hot

Terrain

Solid   Liquid   Gas

Flying mode

Look out for:

Aurora borealis   Spy plane

WELCOME TO THE PLACE THAT LETS LIFE ON EARTH HAPPEN

ATMOSPHERE

GET UP IN THE AIR

The edge of space
The thermosphere is the last layer before space. The air is very thin here.

Natural light
These light displays are called the aurora borealis, or northern lights. Light displays in the southern hemisphere are called the aurora australis.

THE ATMOSPHERE

THE PLACE BETWEEN EARTH AND SPACE

▶ Distance from the surface of the Earth: 0–1,000 km (0–621 miles)

The first Earth feature that you'll come across on your journey is the atmosphere – a layer of gas that protects our planet from the fierce rays of the Sun. Our atmosphere contains the oxygen and carbon dioxide that allow life on Earth, and it stops water from flying off into space. Wear an oxygen mask if you venture outside the ship – the air is only breathable close to Earth.

Eyes in the sky
Spy planes fly high above the clouds to avoid being noticed.

The bands of the **atmosphere** have very different temperatures. Heading up from **Earth** it gets **colder, warmer,** colder again, then warmer again.

CHANGING GASES

Earth's atmosphere has changed several times since it formed. The original atmosphere was mainly made up of volcanic gases, but the atmosphere you'll see today has been altered by life forms and contains more oxygen.

Burning up
Most meteors are vaporized in the atmosphere long before they get near the ground.

The icy layer
This layer has an average temperature of -85°C (-120°F). It is called the mesosphere.

Hot and cold
This layer is called the stratosphere. It is warm at the top and cold at the bottom.

Keeping low
Most passenger planes fly just above the clouds.

The weather layer
All weather happens in the bottom layer of the atmosphere, which is called the troposphere.

CLIMATES

When you explore Earth you'll find it's cold at the poles and hot around the equator. Movement of gas and water in the atmosphere helps create climates – some areas are so hot and dry that deserts form.

Look out
Weather balloons record temperature and pressure.

YOU ARE HERE

ATMOSPHERE

CRUST

MANTLE

CORE

The temperature in the **atmosphere** can get as low as **-120°C** (-184°F) and as high as **1500°C** (2732°F).

Aurora explorer
Travel to the poles at night to observe the northern lights.

Constant companion
Look out for the Moon as it orbits Earth.

ENTER THE
ATMOSPHERE

The atmosphere is not the same all the way through – you'll pass through several layers on your way towards Earth from space. The first layer you'll come across is the thermosphere. While you're here, keep an eye out for the northern lights – flares of light that occur near the poles. The next layer down will be the mesosphere, the coldest part of the whole atmosphere. Further down again is the stratosphere, then finally you'll reach the troposphere, the layer closest to Earth.

Cloud cover
Clouds in the bottom of the atmosphere can obscure the view of Earth from space.

Meteor

Also called shooting stars, meteors are rocks from space. Look for them being vaporized in the layer of the atmosphere called the mesosphere. Very few are big enough to actually reach Earth.

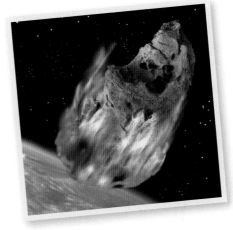

Weather balloons

These balloons fly in the stratosphere, above the troposphere that contains weather. They measure temperature and pressure, letting people on Earth predict the weather.

There is **no solid edge** to the atmosphere – it simply **fades** into space.

THE WEATHER LAYER

All weather happens in the very bottom layer of the atmosphere, which is called the troposphere. Weather systems in this layer create tornadoes, winds, rain, and hail – it can be quite bumpy on the way through!

YOU ARE HERE

ATMOSPHERE

CRUST

MANTLE

CORE

SKYDIVE A
THUNDERSTORM

Thunderstorms happen when moisture and rising warm air combine, with explosive effect. Look for them in hot, wet places such as the southeastern United States, in spring or summer. An average thunderstorm lasts 30 minutes and is about 24 km (15 miles) wide. Some thunderstorms create winds of over 160 kph (100 mph). Strap on a parachute to take a closer look, but be careful – it's stormy out there!

Thunder and **lightning** happen at the same time – you see lightning **before you hear thunder** because light travels faster than sound.

Chase a rainbow

Rainbows are made of light – they form opposite the Sun when it shines through rain.

"I ran for hours and got no closer to it!"

Loud clap
The sound of thunder is made by the movement of air after lightning has struck.

Heavy weather
Thunderstorms often include rain, or frozen balls of water called hail. Some hailstones can be as big as golf balls.

Forked lightning
Not all lightning takes the most straightforward path – some branches out on its way to Earth. It's well worth looking out for!

Sheet lightning
Lightning can jump from cloud to cloud as well as between clouds and the Earth. Keep your eyes peeled, as it's harder to spot.

Building charge
Small pieces of ice in the cloud crash against each other, creating electrical charges inside the cloud.

Hot stuff
Try not to go too close to the lightning – it's eight times hotter than the surface of the Sun!

Light electric
Lightning is visible electrical currents moving between a cloud and the ground.

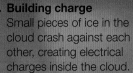

YOU ARE HERE

ATMOSPHERE

CRUST

MANTLE

CORE

FLY THROUGH A
TORNADO

This one is for serious thrill seekers – take a trip through a powerful rotating column of air. Tornadoes form under thunderclouds, with the rotating funnel coming down from the cloud to create devastation on the ground. The most impressive tornadoes occur in the United States, usually in the late afternoon. This is your best chance to catch one, but you'll have to be quick – they usually only last a few minutes.

Lightning bolt
Tornadoes are often accompanied by lightning.

Unfortunate cow
Powerful tornadoes can pick up heavy objects, including livestock, such as cattle.

HEAVY WEATHER

If you'd like to experience a truly incredible storm, look for a hurricane. Also called tropical cyclones, these furious spirals develop over warm water. They have a quiet eye at the centre, with a number of thunderstorms whirling around it.

COLUMNS OF WATER

Tornadoes aren't stuck on land – they can move over water too. Head to the Mediterranean to look for these "waterspouts", but pack some swimming goggles, as these are twisting tubes of water!

YOU ARE HERE

ATMOSPHERE

CRUST

MANTLE

CORE

THE CRUST

Temperature

Cold   Hot

Terrain

Solid   Liquid   Gas

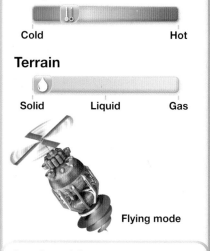

Flying mode

Look out for:

Pumice

Sandstone

EARTH'S OUTER SURFACE

▶ Distance from the surface of the Earth: **0 km (0 miles)**

The crust is the part of the Earth we are most familiar with. It is Earth's solid outer layer. The crust and the top layer of the mantle form a thin rocky shell called the lithosphere, which is broken into sections called tectonic plates. They may seem stable to us, but these plates constantly shift around, thanks to the mobility of the deeper mantle beneath them.

Water world
Oceans cover 70 per cent of Earth's crust.

Hot spot
Pockets of liquid rock called magma can collect above mantle plumes, then bubble up to the surface, where they become solid and create new islands.

Island trail
Island chains form when a plate moves over a stationary hot spot, and new land appears at each location.

Mantle plume
Areas in the mantle where hot rock moves upwards are called mantle plumes.

EYES IN THE SKY

Satellites sit outside Earth's atmosphere and can photograph it from all angles. One way to get a look at the whole of the planet is by joining up satellite images – or jump on board the International Space Station for the view of a lifetime!

The **crust** makes up **less** than **1** per cent of Earth's **volume**. Comparing the **Earth** to an **apple**, the **crust** is as thin as the apple's **skin!**

ATMOSPHERE

YOU ARE HERE

CRUST

MANTLE

CORE

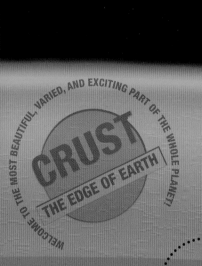

WELCOME TO THE MOST BEAUTIFUL, VARIED, AND EXCITING PART OF THE WHOLE PLANET!

CRUST
THE EDGE OF EARTH

Crust
The crust is a thin shell of rock that forms Earth's outermost layer.

Subduction zone
The crust and the top of the mantle combine to make the tectonic plates that cover Earth's surface. Where these plates meet, one can be pushed under the other, creating a subduction zone.

Mantle
The layer underneath Earth's crust is the mantle, which is made of rock.

Liquid rock
When one plate is pushed under another it slowly melts, creating pockets of liquid rock called magma.

Mammoth mountain
At 8,842 m (29,029 ft) above sea level, Mount Everest towers over everthing else. A skyscraper the same height would have 44,240 storeys! ......

Too high for humans
Heights above 8,000 m (26,200 ft) are known as "the death zone" because of the lack of oxygen. An oxygen mask is essential at this altitude.

A GREAT LEAP!

Soar down from Everest on the paragliding trip of a lifetime.

Cloudtop view
Everest is tall enough to poke out above the clouds.

Carry as much **rubbish away** with you as you can, to **keep** the **mountain** habitat **clean.**

TOUCHDOWN ON
EVEREST

Climbing Mount Everest, the highest peak on Earth's surface, is a tough challenge. Danger is everywhere, with avalanches, cracks in the ice, and extreme cold. Luckily our craft can set you right down on the summit, where you can enjoy stunning views above the cloud tops of the Himalayan mountains.

ATMOSPHERE

YOU ARE HERE

CRUST

MANTLE

CORE

CLIMB TO THE SUMMIT

If you're feeling adventurous, why not land at the base and climb to the top. There are a number of different routes, and some are harder than others. The South route is generally thought to be easiest, but it still has many obstacles such as the Khumbu Icefalls.

RIVERS OF ICE

There are several glaciers close to Everest. The most notable of these is the Rongbuk Glacier, which also serves as base camp for climbers taking the northern approach to Everest. This key site should not be missed, and comes with the added benefit of a spectacular view of the mountain itself.

icy free dive

You need to swim to get to the bottom of some crevasses – wrap up warm under your drysuit!

You could fit **1,600 lorries** in the **largest crevasses.** That's 10 lorries deep, 8 wide, and 20 long!

Climb carefully
Make sure you rope yourself to the top of the glacier before making your descent into a crevasse.

CLIMB DOWN A
CREVASSE

Glaciers are rivers of ice, which are crisscrossed by cracks that form when they flow over uneven ground. These cracks are called crevasses. They are wider at the top than at the bottom and are fascinating for intrepid explorers. However, they are very dangerous to anyone trying to travel across the glacier, as they are often almost invisible due to being covered in snow. Enjoy yourself, but make sure you look where you're putting your feet!

Carved by nature
Some glaciers can form beautiful shapes as they flow along.

Kite skiing
Take advantage of the snow by strapping on some skis and a kite harness for the ride of your life. Make sure to look out for cracks in the glacier.

Snowmobile tours
There's more to see around here than just crevasses – hire a snowmobile for a fast-paced tour around the whole glacier. Some glaciers are hundreds of kilometres long!

TOURIST TIPS

"Watch out"
"Walking out to look at one crevasse, I fell straight into another that was hidden under the snow. Luckily it was a small one and I was able to clamber out."

Activity: Crevasse explorer

"Tricky climb"
"Climbing into the crevasse was easy, but getting out was hard – you'll need to remember ice axes and spikes for your feet. Without them you'll get very stuck!"

Activity: Crevasse explorer

ATMOSPHERE

YOU ARE HERE

CRUST

MANTLE

CORE

HIKE UNDER A
GLACIER

Sheets of ice cover a tenth of Earth's land. In mountainous areas, great tongues of ice creep slowly downhill, inching forwards like rivers in slow motion. Though solid on top, these glaciers are riddled with meltwater channels and grottoes underneath. It's an amazing place to explore, lit by the eerie blue glow of light filtering through the ice.

Watch out for **huge bubbles** of water trapped in the **roof** of ice caves – they may **burst** and shower you with **icy water.**

CLIMB EVEREST

the hard way – under the Khumbu Glacier.

"The experience of a lifetime."
Glacial Times

Camping gear
It's fairly safe to camp under slow-moving glaciers, but avoid more active glaciers as caves may collapse without warning.

DON'T MISS

River of ice

From above, a glacier looks like a river of ice. Rubble and grit stick to the base of the flowing ice, which scrapes away at the ground like a giant piece of sandpaper. As a result, glaciers slowly gouge out huge, steep-sided valleys, reshaping the landscape.

Ice-age relics

Thousands of years ago, Earth was colder and glaciers covered more of the land. You can see evidence of the Ice Age in many places. In Yosemite Valley in the US, for instance, there are huge boulders called "erratics" that were left behind after the ice melted.

ATMOSPHERE

YOU ARE HERE

CRUST

Ice formations
Meltwater can carve the ice into beautiful shapes as it trickles over the roof of an ice cave.

Warm clothing
It's not only freezing under glaciers but often wet too, so bring warm and waterproof clothing.

TOP TIPS

Light fantastic

"Magical"

"Bring a powerful torch to light up the ice. It's like being inside a gigantic jewel!"

Attraction: Ice caving

Under the ice

"Spooky"

"Strange creaking and groaning sounds come from all around. The noise is ice cracking and crunching as the glacier heaves downhill."

Attraction: Glacier tour

MANTLE

CORE

EARTH'S CRUST

The easiest way to get deep into Earth's crust is to explore an area of limestone. Over thousands of years, this sedimentary rock gets eaten away by rain, creating a maze of caverns, tunnels, and underground rivers. It's an exciting but deadly environment, and you'll need excellent climbing skills to explore it.

Cave entrance
The entrance hole to this cave formed when a part of the thin roof collapsed inwards.

Rock bands
Sedimentary rock such as limestone is made of horizontal layers called strata.

Abseiling
Seated in a harness, the climber passes the rope through a metal hoop to slide down slowly.

Most limestone forms from the **shells** of **tiny** sea creatures that pile up on the **seafloor** and eventually **turn into rock.**

TOURIST TIP

Rope descent

"Hair-raising"

"The only way to the bottom of some caves is to abseil down a rope. You'll need nerves of steel to do this. Take a helmet light so you can see the cave floor, but don't look down too often!"

Attraction: Abseiling

CAVE LIFE

Some animals have adapted to life in dark, damp caves and live there permanently. Because there's no light, these animals have become blind and colourless over hundreds of thousands of years. The skin of the ghostly looking blind cave fish is almost see-through.

Cave diving

Take a scuba safari through the fabulous flooded caverns of Mexico.

"The nearest thing to being in outer space!"
News of the Underworld

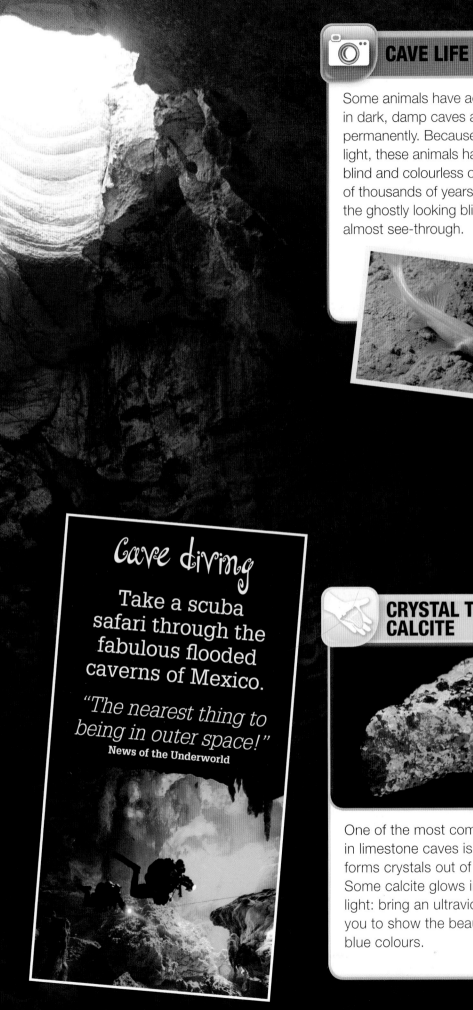

CRYSTAL TIPS: CALCITE

One of the most common minerals in limestone caves is calcite, which forms crystals out of dripping water. Some calcite glows in ultraviolet light: bring an ultraviolet light with you to show the beautiful pink and blue colours.

ATMOSPHERE

YOU ARE HERE

CRUST

MANTLE

CORE

25

Mammoth hunt

Head north to hunt for mammoths, which have been hidden under the ice for thousands of years!

Hold tight
Fossil hunting can be dangerous work – make sure you have all the safety equipment you need before tackling the tougher locations.

Hard to get at
Fossils are often very deeply embedded in rock – getting them out takes the patience and hard work of dedicated experts.

ANCIENT ROCKS

Deep layers of rock are older than higher ones, and different fossils can be found in each layer. Make sure to look at the rock around you while you're fossil hunting. Scientists use big events like ice ages to work out how old rocks are, then they can find out how old the types of fossils in the rocks are.

HUNT FOR
FOSSILS

Get some clues about how Earth looked millions of years ago by looking at fossils that have been left behind in the rock. Fossils form in very particular circumstances, when an animal or plant dies and is quickly covered over with soil rather than rotting away. Over time, the remains turn into solid rock and are preserved as fossils. There are many types of fossil, from huge dinosaurs to bacteria that are too small to see with the naked eye. Get out there and see what you can find!

Rocky treasure
Fossils are irreplaceable – excavation must be done very carefully. Wear protective clothing to make sure nothing contaminates your finds.

The **biggest** known **dinosaur** is **Argentinosaurus.** It was **five** times **taller** than an **elephant!**

ATMOSPHERE

YOU ARE HERE

CRUST

MANTLE

CORE

GREAT FINDS

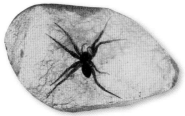

Amber
Fossilized tree sap is called amber. It often contains the remains of insects unfortunate enough to have got trapped in the sticky sap before it hardened.

Ammonite
These shells contained creatures related to octopuses. They swam around in the sea, rather than having to stay on rocks and plants like snails.

Cool suit
You will need to wear a suit packed with ice cubes, as temperatures can reach a sweltering 50°C (122°F)!

GO FOR IT!
Dive down an underground waterfall.

Gypsum giant
Some gypsum crystals can grow up to 15 m (50 ft) long.

EXPLORE A CRYSTAL CAVERN

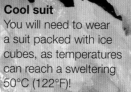

Visit the incredible crystal cavern and see for yourself why these super-sized gems are the number one crust attraction. Crystals grow when hot water cools and minerals from the water become solid. The slower the water cools, the bigger the crystals can become. Inside Earth's crust huge caverns can form, filled with enormous shimmering crystals.

Don't take your oxygen **mask off.** The air in the cavern is **extremely hot and humid** and you will find it very difficult to breathe.

28

Cave exploration

"Awesome!"
"The crystal cave was the most incredible thing I've ever seen. Some of the crystals were bigger than buses!"

Activity: Crystal tour

Tricky viewing

"Too hot"
"It was pretty, but really hot and wet – it was hard work climbing over the crystals. I wish I'd just looked at the photos."

Activity: Crystal tour

📷 CAVE OF SWORDS

This cave's walls are covered with sparkling crystals, which all stick out from its sides. Each crystal is about 1 m (3 ft) long. Take a look at this spectacular cave, but be careful not to get too close to its sharp sides!

ATMOSPHERE

YOU ARE HERE

CRUST

MANTLE

CORE

Deep down
This cave is 300 m (980 ft) underground.

HOLDING TIGHT

Squeeze down a pothole into a limestone cave to hunt for these incredible formations. Stalactites hang from the roof of a cave – they form when minerals solidify from water filtering through the rock above. Stalagmites are made from the drips that fall off the stalactites. They're well worth a photo!

TOURIST TIPS

Narrow squeeze

"Amazing journey"
"We followed the underground river down tunnels that were really small – at one point I was worried we'd run out of air. It was pretty exciting though!"

Activity: Underground explorer

Eyes up
Look for stalactites hanging down from the roofs of caves.

Carry on down

Keep exploring – go farther underground on the cave dive of a lifetime!

Cave paintings
Some caves contain paintings made up to 40,000 years ago – keep an eye out for these prehistoric relics.

Bats
Underground tunnels contain various wildlife – look out especially for bats that sleep upside down in caves during the day.

ATMOSPHERE

YOU ARE HERE

CRUST

Water transport
There are many travel options here – you could swim, scuba, kayak, or even take an underwater scooter.

MANTLE

SAIL AN UNDERGROUND
RIVER

CORE

Many of Earth's rivers do not simply meander along the surface. Some stay entirely underground, others only dip underground for part of their length. Follow a river on its journey into the Earth, and keep your eyes open – there's a lot to see. You may be able to disembark in some areas for a look down smaller tunnels – mind your head!

Explosive entertainment

"Amazing!"

"I watched islands forming when volcanoes erupted as plates moved together. It was brilliant – there was lava everywhere!"

Activity: Tectonic tour

Do your research

"Boring"

"We wanted to see volcanoes, but the plate we were looking at didn't do much. Do your research and make sure you visit the right plate!"

Activity: Plate watching

Dive in a deep sea trench

Discover new land being created as plates pull apart under the sea.

250 million years ago **tectonic plates** brought all the world's land together into one **continent,** called **Pangea.**

Transform boundary
Ridges like this one are created when plates move past each other.

COLLISION ZONE

Earth's surface is not fixed in one solid piece – it is made up of sections, called tectonic plates. The plates sit on top of the Earth's mantle, which slowly moves, pushing the plates around. They are always moving, but very slowly, at about the speed that hair grows. Find the edge of a plate to get the best views of tectonic activity – see where plates slip under each other, push together, or slide along next to each other. This is the Earth in action!

ATMOSPHERE

YOU ARE HERE

CRUST

MANTLE

CORE

San Andreas Fault
This fault line is in California, in the United States. It is about 810 miles (1300 km) long.

ON THE GROUND

Pushing together
Look out for where plates push together – one is forced under the other, causing the land to buckle, and volcanoes and mountains like the Himalayas can be created.

Pulling apart
The East African Rift Valley was formed where plates pulled apart, creating new land between them.

TECTONIC PLATES

Earth's crust is divided into tectonic plates, which are always on the move. The boundaries where plates meet can be quite dramatic. Plates are usually thin under oceans and thicker under land.

WITNESS AN
EARTHQUAKE

Earth's surface is not as immobile as it might seem. It moves constantly, pushed around by movements in the mantle beneath. Earthquakes are caused where the tectonic plates that make up Earth's surface collide or rub against each other. This movement creates strong vibrations that make the ground shake. Earthquakes can reshape the surface and create serious damage, especially in cities. Earthquakes occur along the edges of Earth's tectonic plates.

Big vibrations
The vibrations created by earthquakes can cause a lot of damage, especially in built-up areas.

Cracking up
Some earthquakes are strong enough to break the ground right open.

Built to last
Modern buildings in earthquake-prone areas are designed to move with the ground during earthquakes, so they don't fall over.

THE QUAKE'S CENTRE

Each earthquake centres around an underground focus point, often created by the plates rubbing against each other. The most damage to the crust occurs right above this focus, in a place called the epicentre. The vibrations are strongest at the epicentre.

Moving plates

Epicentre

Vibrations

Focus

The **biggest earthquake** ever **recorded** was in **Chile** in **1960.** It created ocean **waves** that were over **10 m** (35 ft) **tall.**

THE EARTH MOVES

Earthquakes can make the ground move in unexpected ways. There is a deafening noise, the Earth shakes, and buildings can fall over. Most earthquakes only last for a few minutes.

ATMOSPHERE

YOU ARE HERE

CRUST

MANTLE

CORE

SKATE THROUGH A
LAVA TUBE

For an incredible sporting experience, hunt out a lava tube. These rocky tunnels are left behind when the lava that once flowed along them has drained out. Lava tubes come in many different shapes and sizes. If you can find a circular tube it's like skating nature's half-pipe! If you find a bumpy tube try an all-terrain mountain bike for a fast and exciting ride.

Lava explorer

Grab a super-strong unmeltable kayak to get an up-close look at fresh, free-flowing lava.

All shapes and sizes
Lava tubes are not all the same shape – they vary depending on how the lava that formed them was flowing.

The world's **longest lava tube** is Kazamura Cave in **Hawaii,** which is 65 km (40 miles) long – that's the same as 160 times round a running track.

TOURIST TIPS

Skating adventure

"Great skate"

"I normally skate at my local park – this was a thousand times better and I can't wait to do it again!"

★★★★☆

Activity: Lava-tube skating

BOMBS AWAY

Volcanoes throw out hard lumps of rock as well as liquid lava. When you're exploring a volcanic area it's a good idea to wear a helmet and keep a watchful eye on the skies!

Sporting opportunities
These natural tubes offer the perfect location for all sorts of sports. Roller-skating and skate-boarding are just two of the many things you could try.

ATMOSPHERE

YOU ARE HERE

CRUST

MANTLE

CORE

HOT CRYSTALS

Look out for mineral crystals appearing around the edges of the magma chamber. These form when the hot, liquid rock starts to cool down. The first crystals to form will often be a green mineral called olivine.

Way out
When the pressure in the chamber builds, the magma will push to the surface in a volcanic eruption.

Unstable cave
Some of the magma in this chamber has drained down into the mantle. Enjoy the cavern, but watch out as the roof could collapse at any minute!

Liquid rock
Magma is very hot molten rock.

Super heated
Make sure you wear a safety suit – temperatures can top 1,000°C (1,800°F)!

Non-event

"Not worth the trip"

"The only magma chamber we found had never exploded, so the magma had hardened into rock. Still, we did see lots of granite!"

★☆☆☆☆

Activity type: Rock tour

Liquid rock is called **magma** while it is **under** the **surface** of the Earth, but **lava above** Earth's surface.

SPEED ACROSS A
MAGMA LAKE

Drill down into Earth's crust to splash around in the liquid heart of a volcano – a magma chamber. These chambers are home to pockets of molten rock, which are created by movement in the mantle below. If the pressure in a magma chamber rises high enough, its magma can burst to Earth's surface in a volcanic eruption. You need to enter a chamber very carefully, because any sudden change in its environment could trigger a volcanic eruption that will shoot you out of the crust.

ATMOSPHERE

YOU ARE HERE

CRUST

MANTLE

CORE

Lava

Volcanoes spew out red-hot, liquid rock called lava in tall jets and also as more slow-moving streams. One of the best places to get a close look at some lava is Hawaii.

Ground gas

Volcanoes can create ground-level clouds of hot gas and rock particles called pyroclastic flows. They are extremely dangerous, so it's best to watch from a distance.

Mighty ship
Stay safe inside the ship, which can withstand incredible heat.

Rocky fountain
Volcanoes can shoot liquid rock called lava high up into the sky.

Volcanic **eruptions** can create enormous clouds of **gas,** which can **rise** over **30 km** (17 miles) high.

Lava flow
The rivers of lava created by volcanoes can flow for long distances. Eventually they cool and turn into rock.

FLY OUT OF A VOLCANO

Volcanoes are formed where molten rock called magma rises up through the Earth to escape through the crust. There are many types of volcano – they can be huge and explosive or small and steady. Some erupt continuously, others go many years between eruptions or stop erupting altogether. Drill down into the magma chamber under a volcano that's ready to blow and get ready for the ride of a lifetime!

RING OF FIRE

If you want to get as many volcanoes in as possible, take a trip to the Pacific Ocean to visit the Ring of Fire. The Pacific Rim contains 75 per cent of the world's volcanoes!

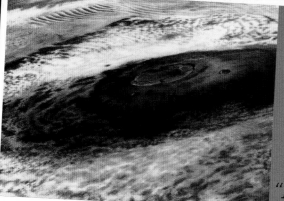

MARTIAN GIANT

Visit Mars to see Olympus Mons, the biggest volcano in the Solar System.

"It was out of this world!"

ATMOSPHERE

YOU ARE HERE

CRUST

MANTLE

CORE

CRUISE THE OCEAN FLOOR

The ocean floor is immense, and almost as varied as land. There's a lot worth seeing down here, from underwater canyons to newly formed sea floor. The movement of tectonic plates has a lot of impact on how the ocean floor looks – it creates underground mountains and chains of volcanic islands. Enjoy your cruise, but keep your eyes peeled – there's a lot to get in!

Swim with sharks!

Take a dip with the ocean's most popular predators!

Topless mountain
These flat-topped underwater mountains are called guyots.

Sloping floor
The ocean floor is not flat – it has many sections at different heights.

Heavy boots
Make sure you add weights to your boots if you would like to walk on the ocean floor – otherwise you'll float off!

OCEAN LIFE

The ocean is full of animals, from huge whales down to tiny plankton. Look around to see what you can find, as there's a lot of variety. This massive Whale Shark only eats small creatures, such as krill and young fish.

There are over a **million** species of **plants** and **animals** in the **ocean.** Scientists think there are another **nine** million species waiting to be **discovered.**

THE LAYERED SEA

You'll find that everything looks quite different as you descend through the ocean – it will get much darker as you get deeper, and the pressure will increase. Animals have adapted to live at different depths.

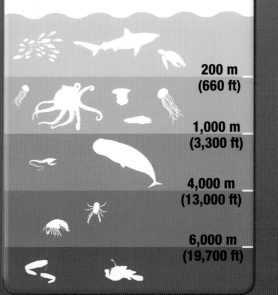

200 m (660 ft)

1,000 m (3,300 ft)

4,000 m (13,000 ft)

6,000 m (19,700 ft)

Shine a light
No sunlight reaches this deep into the ocean – use the ship's light to see the ocean floor.

New land
Mid-ocean ridges are created where two plates pull away from each other, and magma bubbles up in between. The magma hardens into new sea floor.

ATMOSPHERE

YOU ARE HERE

CRUST

MANTLE

CORE

BLACK SMOKER

Black smokers were only discovered in 1977, but they're now open to visitors all year round. They form where cold water seeps down through cracks in the newly formed ocean floor. It gets heated and rises, flowing back into the main ocean. Minerals like iron and calcium that were dissolved in the water then solidify, creating tall chimneys around plumes of black or white liquid. This is one of the most spectacular sights in the ocean!

Let off some steam

Take a tour of a geyser field to see how super-heated water behaves above ground.

"This blew my mind!"

Hot water
You'll be more comfortable observing from a distance, as the water is very hot. Only the weight of water above stops it from boiling.

Unique life
Some animals have evolved to live in these difficult environments.

LIFE IN THE DEEP

You can find some very unusual fish at the bottom of the sea. It is dark, with high pressure and cold water. Fish like this fangtooth have evolved to survive in these extreme conditions. They are interesting but hard to find – many are as black as the water around them.

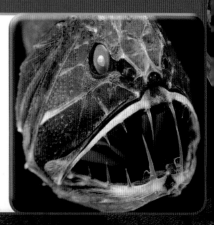

📷 VENT LIFE

Areas around black smokers are so far from the ocean surface that there are no plants. Instead, animals like these tube worms have evolved to live on chemical energy. Look out for vent shrimp and scaly foot snails.

Black smoker
The plumes of liquid rising from the vents can be either white or black.

The deepest known **black smokers** are **5,000 m (16,500 ft) under** the **sea.** That's the same as 10 Empire State Buildings on top of each other.

ATMOSPHERE

YOU ARE HERE

CRUST

MANTLE

CORE

NEED TO KNOW

Temperature

Cold   Hot

Terrain

Solid   Liquid   Gas

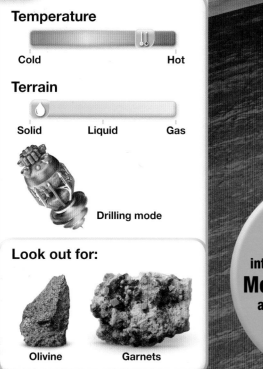

Drilling mode

Look out for:

Olivine   Garnets

Earth is not the only planet to be divided into **layers – Mars, Mercury, and Venus** are all thought to have **rock mantles.**

Crust
Above the mantle is the crust, a thin shell of rock that forms Earth's surface.

THE MANTLE

EARTH'S THICKEST LAYER

▶ Distance from the surface of the Earth: **2,900 km (1,800 miles)**

The mantle is the thickest of Earth's layers. It sits under the crust and is made of solid rock. Although the rock in the mantle is solid, the high pressure and temperature inside Earth mean that it moves, though usually incredibly slowly. Towards the top of the mantle, pockets of liquid rock called magma can form, and can then come to the surface as lava. This is a vast and largely unexplored region.

HEAT SOURCES

The heat inside Earth comes from two different sources. Some is left over from the formation of the Earth, billions of years ago. The rest is thought to be caused by radioactive elements like uranium and thorium breaking into smaller pieces. A lead-lined suit will help protect you from the radiation here.

Mantle
Earth's mantle is a solid rocky layer, between the crust and the core. It makes up 80 per cent of Earth's volume.

WELCOME TO THE MANTLE – IT'S SOLID BUT CONSTANTLY ON THE MOVE!

MANTLE
THE ROCKY LAYER

Outer core
Beneath the mantle is the outer core. This layer is a liquid, made of a mixture of iron and sulphur.

POWER UP!
Keep an eye out for traces of uranium in the mantle – one kilo (2 lbs) can produce as much energy as 3,000 tonnes of coal!

ATMOSPHERE

CRUST

YOU ARE HERE

MANTLE

CORE

DIVE UNDER THE CRUST

The mantle is not the same all the way through – scientists think that it is as varied as the crust above it. Some parts of the mantle are cooler than others, and pockets of magma can develop where it's hottest. Mantle rock is steadily but constantly on the move. In some places old pieces of plate can slip right down into the mantle. Dive down under the crust to explore this highly varied environment.

TOURIST TIPS

"Exciting journey"
"I liked seeing that the mantle isn't all the same – our ship got caught in a pocket of magma for a while! Luckily we were able to use the ship's propellers to get through."

Activity: Mantle exploration

Melting away
Pockets of liquid rock called magma are formed as plates melt into the mantle.

Plate in the mantle
Pieces of tectonic plates can get pushed down into the mantle, where they steadily melt.

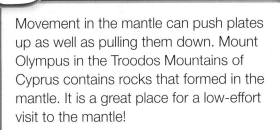

MANTLE AT THE TOP

Movement in the mantle can push plates up as well as pulling them down. Mount Olympus in the Troodos Mountains of Cyprus contains rocks that formed in the mantle. It is a great place for a low-effort visit to the mantle!

Visit the Farallon plate

This plate has slipped under North America – come and take a look at plate tectonics in action!

"An eye-opening experience."
The Mantle Times

ATMOSPHERE

CRUST

YOU ARE HERE

MANTLE

CORE

PUSHY PLATES

The plates that make up Earth's surface can push under each other. The edge of one plate rides up and over the other, forcing it down into the mantle, where it gradually melts. Mountains form where the top plate folds up as the plates collide. Volcanoes can be created where liquid rock bubbles up from the mantle to Earth's surface.

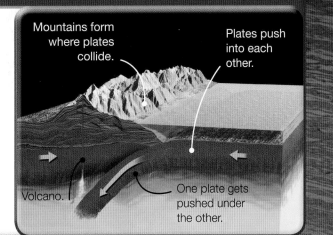

Mountains form where plates collide.

Plates push into each other.

Volcano.

One plate gets pushed under the other.

Rocky bubble
Pockets of liquid magma can form at the top of the mantle plume, and sometimes find their way to Earth's surface.

Hot spot
Mantle plumes are hotter and therefore less dense than the rock around them, which is why they move upwards.

Breaking through
The heat at the top of a plume can melt through the crust above.

Rocky ride
The rock you're on may be moving, but the rock around you might not be – keep your elbows in!

Rock on the move
Just because there are currents in the mantle doesn't mean that it's liquid. The solid rock moves because it's under extreme pressure.

The **mantle** is **solid** but it can **flow** very **slowly**. **Currents** in the mantle move at the same speed your **fingernails grow**.

ISLAND CHAINS

Why not do a little island hopping? Scientists believe that hot spots in the mantle can melt through the crust, letting magma bubble up and harden. Where the crust is moving this can create chains of small islands, such as Hawaii, in the Pacific Ocean.

TOURIST TIPS

"Dull ride"

"We thought this sounded amazing, but actually mantle rock moves really slowly. I've heard that the currents in the outer core are a lot more interesting."

"Too hot"

"Nice idea, but it's hot in the mantle – I couldn't really enjoy myself because I was sweating too much. I'm looking forward to getting back to the ship."

Attraction type: Ride

RIDE A MANTLE
PLUME

The mantle is always on the move. As you drill through it, look out for areas of hot rock moving up and areas of cooler rock moving down. Areas where hot rock moves up are called mantle plumes, but no-one knows much about them. If you find one, you might be able to catch a lift to the crust, or you could surf back down against the flow to discover just how deep it goes. You'll need a time machine for this adventure – the mantle moves very slowly and your ride could last for 100 million years!

ATMOSPHERE

CRUST

YOU ARE HERE

MANTLE

CORE

HUNT FOR DIAMONDS

Diamonds form between 150 and 190 kilometers (90–120 miles) underneath Earth's crust, in the mantle. They are brought to Earth's surface by volcanic eruptions, but not all volcanic eruptions throw out lava that contains diamonds. Try a different approach to diamond hunting by looking for them here, in the mantle itself. This is a once-in-a-lifetime opportunity that shouldn't be missed!

Hidden treasure
Diamonds form in Earth's mantle. For your best chance of finding them, you'll need to drill down more than 150 kilometers (90 miles) from the surface.

BAG A GEODE

Can't find diamonds? Try quartz instead. Hunt for crystal-packed, sparkling cavities in Earth's crust.

COLOURED GEMS

Only the most perfect diamonds are transparent. Most contain chemical impurities that give a coloured tint – they can be almost any colour, including pink, yellow, red, and green.

Solid tunnel
The mantle is made of solid rock, so your ship will leave a tunnel behind as it drills downward.

Mighty drill
The ship's drill has to be incredibly strong to get through the rock.

ATMOSPHERE

CRUST

YOU ARE HERE

MANTLE

CORE

53

THE CORE

THE HOTTEST PLACE IN EARTH

▶ Distance from the surface of the Earth: **3,200 km (2,000 miles)**

The liquid outer core makes a welcome change of scene after many days spent drilling through the rocky mantle. Set your craft to swim mode to reach the solid inner core that sits at the very centre of the Earth. Temperatures in the core are so hot that your transport could easily melt away around you, so ensure your ship's refrigeration system is set to maximum.

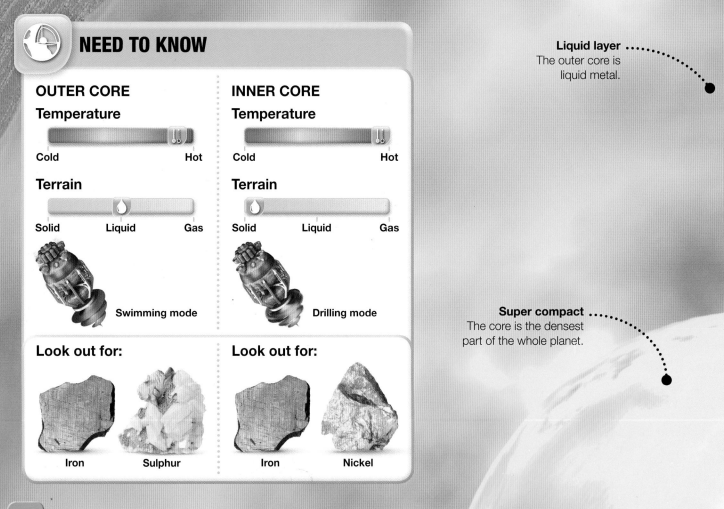

NEED TO KNOW

OUTER CORE

Temperature

Cold ———————————— Hot

Terrain

Solid ——— Liquid ——— Gas

Swimming mode

Look out for:

Iron   Sulphur

INNER CORE

Temperature

Cold ———————————— Hot

Terrain

Solid ——— Liquid ——— Gas

Drilling mode

Look out for:

Iron   Nickel

Liquid layer
The outer core is liquid metal.

Super compact
The core is the densest part of the whole planet.

The **core** is the **same size** as the **planet Mars.** It makes up about **16 per cent of Earth.**

UNDER PRESSURE

The inner core is only solid because the pressure at the centre of the Earth is strong enough to win over temperature, and forces the iron to solidify. You won't want to stay down here for long!

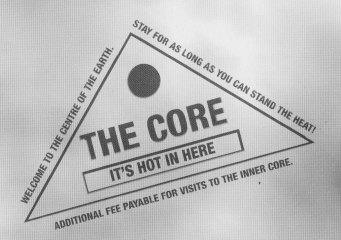

WELCOME TO THE CENTRE OF THE EARTH.

STAY FOR AS LONG AS YOU CAN STAND THE HEAT!

THE CORE
IT'S HOT IN HERE

ADDITIONAL FEE PAYABLE FOR VISITS TO THE INNER CORE.

THE HOTTEST PLACE TO PARTY!

Celebrate! You've made it to the centre of the planet.

Solid core
The inner core is made of solid iron.

ATMOSPHERE

CRUST

MANTLE

YOU ARE HERE

CORE

SAIL THE SEA OF IRON

The outer core is the only area inside Earth that is liquid. This constantly moving sea is not made of water but molten metal – mainly of iron, nickel, and sulphur. Extreme temperatures keep the mixture liquid – it's about 5,000°C (9,000°F) down here! You'll probably want to wear your refrigerated suit inside the vehicle from this point onwards – it's hard to stay cool when it's so hot outside.

Super heated
The metal that makes up the outer core is extremely hot. The sulphur mixed in with the iron and nickel means the mixture stays liquid, unlike the solid metal inner core.

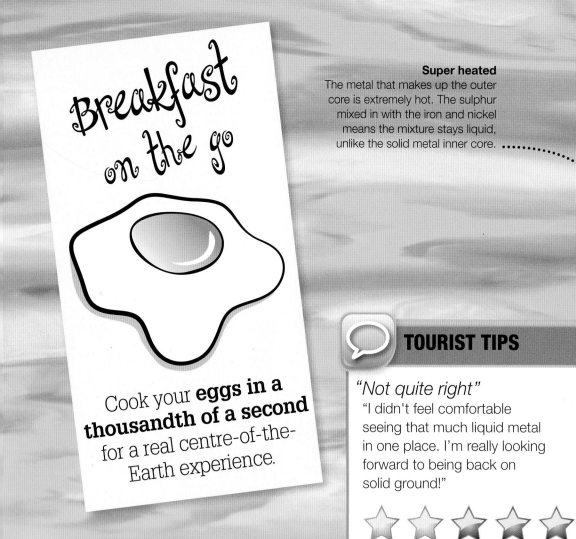

Breakfast on the go

Cook your **eggs in a thousandth of a second** for a real centre-of-the-Earth experience.

TOURIST TIPS

"Not quite right"
"I didn't feel comfortable seeing that much liquid metal in one place. I'm really looking forward to being back on solid ground!"

★★★☆☆

Attraction type: Core tour

FLOWING IRON

Intense heat within the Earth means that there are currents in the outer core. Liquid iron cools where it is near the mantle and then sinks, only to be heated by the inner core and rise again. Even more currents are added by the constant rotation of Earth. It's pretty turbulent, so hold tight!

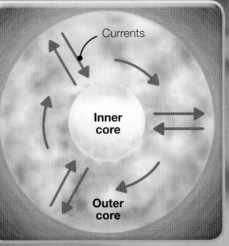

Currents

Inner core

Outer core

Hot stuff
Come outside to have a look, but you won't want to stay in the heat for long. Only the incredible heat-resistant powers of the ship prevent it from melting away.

Set to swim
Make sure your ship is ready for its journey through the molten iron – you'll need the propellers rather than the drill for this trip.

The **liquid outer core** makes up about **30 per cent** of Earth's **mass**. It's **bigger** than the **Moon.**

MAGNETIC PULL

The movement of the molten iron in the outer core creates a magnetic field around Earth. This protects the planet from the Sun's radiation, making life on Earth possible.

Radiation from the Sun

Earth

Magnetic field

ATMOSPHERE

CRUST

MANTLE

YOU ARE HERE

CORE

RIDE THE
MAGNETIC FIELD

Jump onto a giant magnet and hold tight – this will be an exhilarating ride! The constant movement of liquid iron in Earth's turbulent outer core generates a magnetic field that surrounds our planet. This field protects Earth from solar wind, by preserving the atmosphere that prevents harmful radiation from reaching Earth's surface. This magnetic field extends for tens of thousands of kilometres into space around Earth.

Inner core ....
At the very centre of Earth is a solid inner core.

The **magnetic** field allows us to find our way around – the magnet on a **compass** always points to the magnetic **north** pole.

COSMIC RAYS

Harmful radioactive rays are created by supernovas and other objects in the Universe. The magnetic field protects Earth from these cosmic rays. You'll be safe in the core, but be sure to stay away from rays if you visit the outer edges of the magnetic field.

MAGNETIC POLES

The magnetic field loops around Earth, but becomes vertical at two points on opposite sides of Earth. These points are the north and south magnetic poles. They are in slightly different locations from the north and south geographic poles.

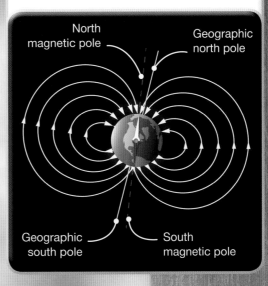

North magnetic pole

Geographic north pole

Geographic south pole

South magnetic pole

Liquid iron
Earth's magnetic field is created by the constant movement of liquid iron in the outer core.

PLAY THE FIELD

Earth's magnetic field flips every 200,000 years or so – get your timing right and reap the rewards!

"I loved it!"
Prehistoric Times

Ride a magnet
Find a magnet to catch a ride on the magnetic field.

ATMOSPHERE

CRUST

MANTLE

YOU ARE HERE

CORE

59

TOUCHDOWN ON THE
INNER CORE

To reach the inner core, you must swim your ship through the sea of molten iron that makes up the outer core. As you near the bottom of this white-hot ocean, watch out for one of the wonders of Earth's interior: a forest of gigantic nickel-iron crystals, each up to 10 km (6 miles) tall, that covers the inner core. Pick your way carefully between these hazards to find a safe landing site.

Giant crystals
Iron and nickel have solidified on the inner core's surface to form towering crystals 100 times taller than skyscrapers.

CRYSTAL GARDEN

Earth's core is a great place to hunt for exotic crystals. They form here because the core is slowly cooling, a process that has been going on for billions of years. Eventually the whole core will become solid and Earth will lose its protective magnetic field. When that happens, harmful rays from the Sun will break into the atmosphere, ending life on Earth.

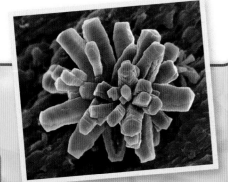

Earth's solid **inner core** gets **1 mm (0.04 in) wider every year** as the crystals **grow** on its surface.

Temperatures soar to **6,000°C** (11,000°F) at the **inner core,** which is as **hot** as the **surface** of the **Sun. Stay inside** your **ship!**

Sail the sea of iron
Your ship must be able to withstand swirling currents and pressures three million times greater than at Earth's surface.

TOURIST TIPS

Zero gravity

"Amazing!"
"It's huge fun at the core because Earth's gravity is equal in all directions, making you weightless, just like in outer space."

⭐⭐⭐⭐⭐

Zero gravity

"Bleh!"
"Bring a supply of sick bags – not everyone enjoys Zero-G."

⭐⭐⭐⭐⭐

Attraction type: Core cruise

MAKE A TRILLION

Search for gold in Earth's core. Scientists estimate there's enough here to cover Earth's surface in a layer of gold 50 cm (20 in) thick.

ATMOSPHERE

CRUST

MANTLE

YOU ARE HERE

CORE

VISIT THE CENTRE OF
THE EARTH

Earth's inner core is a mishmash of enormous crystals, with one gigantic specimen at its very centre. This huge nickel-iron crystal has been gradually growing over billions of years – it is now the biggest crystal in or on Earth, and one of the planet's key visitor attractions. You might want to book in advance – it can get crowded at the core!

TOURIST TIPS

Quiet at the centre

"Huge crystal"
"There wasn't a lot to see at the centre of the Earth – just a big crystal. It is the biggest crystal in the world though!"

Attraction type: Inner core tour

Crystal maze
The inner core is made up of many metal crystals that all interlock with each other.

INNER SPIN

The inner core rotates, turning approximately 0.3 to 0.5 degrees more per year than the rotation of Earth's surface. That's only one extra rotation for every 700–1,000 years though, so you probably won't feel it during your visit!

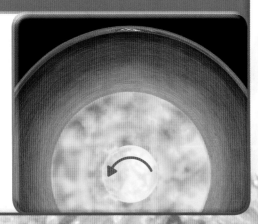

MAKING AN EXIT

To get back to Earth's surface, you'll need to travel back through all its layers. Once you're out of the inner core, sail up through the liquid outer core, then use the drill to get through the mantle and the crust.

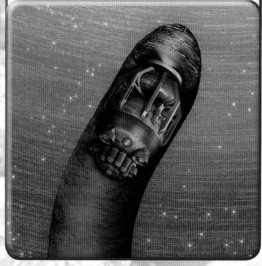

Central giant
The crystal at the centre of the Earth is thought to be 2,400 km (1,500 miles) long!

The **largest** known **crystal** at the surface is **11 m** (36 ft) long – the same length as a double decker **bus!**

Stay indoors
The closer you travel to the centre of the Earth, the hotter it gets. At the very centre temperatures can reach 4,000°C (7,232°F).

ATMOSPHERE

CRUST

MANTLE

YOU ARE HERE

CORE

INDEX

ACKNOWLEDGMENTS

Dorling Kindersley would like to thank Hedi Hunter and Smiljka Surla for additional design support, Steve Willis for retouching images, Chris Bernstein for the index, Scarlett O'Hara for proofreading, Rob Nunn from the picture library, and Sonia Charbonnier for CTS support.

The publisher would like to thank the following for their kind permission to reproduce their photographs:

(Key: a-above; b-below/bottom; c-centre; f-far; l-left; r-right; t-top)

4-5 Corbis: Ocean. 4 Dorling Kindersley: NASA (bl). 6-7 Dorling Kindersley: NASA. 6 Dorling Kindersley: NASA (bl); ShutterStock (bc). 7 SuperStock: National Geographic (cr). 9 SuperStock: Tetra Images (cra); Westend61 (crb). 10 SuperStock: Wayne Lynch / All Canada Photos (tl). 10-11

SuperStock: Fotosearch. 11 Getty Images: Photographer's Choice RF / Images Etc Ltd (cra). Science Photo Library: British Antarctic Survey (crb). SuperStock: age fotostock (br). 12-13 Corbis: Robert Postma / First Light. 12 Dorling Kindersley: Karen Trist / Rough Guides (fcrb). 13 Alamy Images: Horizon International Images Limited (cra). Dorling Kindersley: Karen Trist / Rough Guides (fcl, fclb). SuperStock: Universal Images Group (cla). 15 Getty Images: DEA / C. Andreoli / De Agostini Picture Library (br). NASA: Terra Satellite / EOS (cra). 17 NASA: (tc). 18-19 Dorling Kindersley: Tim Draper / Rough Guides. 19 Getty Images: age fotostock / Santiago Yaniz (br); Aurora / Jake Norton (bl). 20-21 Getty Images: Workbook Stock / Adrian Mueller - Fabrik Studios. 21 Corbis: Marten Dalfors / Naturbild (cr). Getty Images: Aurora / Joe McBride (cra). 22 Getty Images: The Image Bank /

picturegarden (bl). 22-23 Science Photo Library: David Nunuk. 23 Corbis: David Muench (cra). SuperStock: Thomas Kitchin & Victoria Hurst / All Canada Photos (cla). 24-25 Getty Images: National Geographic / Stephen Alvarez. 25 Corbis: Arne Hodalic (cra); Henry Watkins & Yibran Aragon / Reuters (bl). 26 Dorling Kindersley: Jon Hughes & Russell Gooday (tl/mammoth). Getty Images: Digital Vision / Buena Vista Images (tl/forest); Photonica / GK Hart / Vicky Hart (tl/ice); Photographer's Choice / Tim Kiusalaas (br). 26-27 SuperStock: Louie Psihoyos / Science Faction. 28 Getty Images: National Geographic / Stephen Alvarez (tl). 28-29 Getty Images: Carsten Peter / Speleoresearch & Films / National Geographic. 29 Science Photo Library: Javier Trueba / MSF (cr). 30 Alamy Images: Gavin Newman (tc). Getty Images: Photodisc / Keren Su (fcla); Sites &

Photos / Samuel Magal (cla). SuperStock: Stocktrek Images (clb). 30-31 Alamy Images: David Kilpatrick. 31 SuperStock: Minden Pictures (cra); Robert Harding Picture Library (cla). 32 Dorling Kindersley: David Peart (cl). 32-33 Getty Images: Stone / James Balog. 33 Getty Images: age fotostock / Ignacio Palacios (crb); Flickr / Thierry Hennet (br). 35 Getty Images: AFP Photo / Soe Than Win (br). 36-37 Alamy Images: Inga Spence. 37 Getty Images: Flickr / Jeff R. Clow (fcl); Photonica / Connor Walberg (cl). SuperStock: Blend Images (bc, clb); Westend61 (cr). 38 Corbis: Jack Hollingsworth (bl). 40-41 SuperStock: Stocktrek Images. 40 Dorling Kindersley: Greg Ward / Rough Guides (tl). Getty Images: The Image Bank / David Sanger. 41 Dorling Kindersley: NASA / JPL (bl). SuperStock: LatitudeStock (crb). 43 Getty Images: Digital Vision / Justin Lewis (tc). 44 SuperStock: Fancy Collection (clb); Minden Pictures (br). 44-45 Dorling Kindersley: Atlantic Digital. 45 Corbis: Ralph White (tr). 47 Corbis: Alain Nogues / Sygma (cra).

Dorling Kindersley: Natural History Museum, London (crb). 49 Alamy Images: iWebbtravel (cla). 51 Getty Images: Stocktrek Images (cla). 55 Dorling Kindersley: Natural History Museum, London (cra). 56-57 Corbis: Arthur Morris. 58 NASA: JPL-Caltech / STScI / CXC / SAO (bc). 60-61 Science Photo Library: Steve Gschmeissner. 60 Science Photo Library: Steve Gschmeissner. 61 Fotolia: Iraidka (c). 62-63 Dorling Kindersley: Natural History Museum, London. Science Photo Library: Scott Camazine (background). 62 Dorling Kindersley: Satellite Imagemap Copyright / 1996-2003 Planetary Visions (cb).

Front and Back Endpapers: Getty Images: The Image Bank / Werner Van Steen.

All other images © Dorling Kindersley For further information see: www.dkimages.com

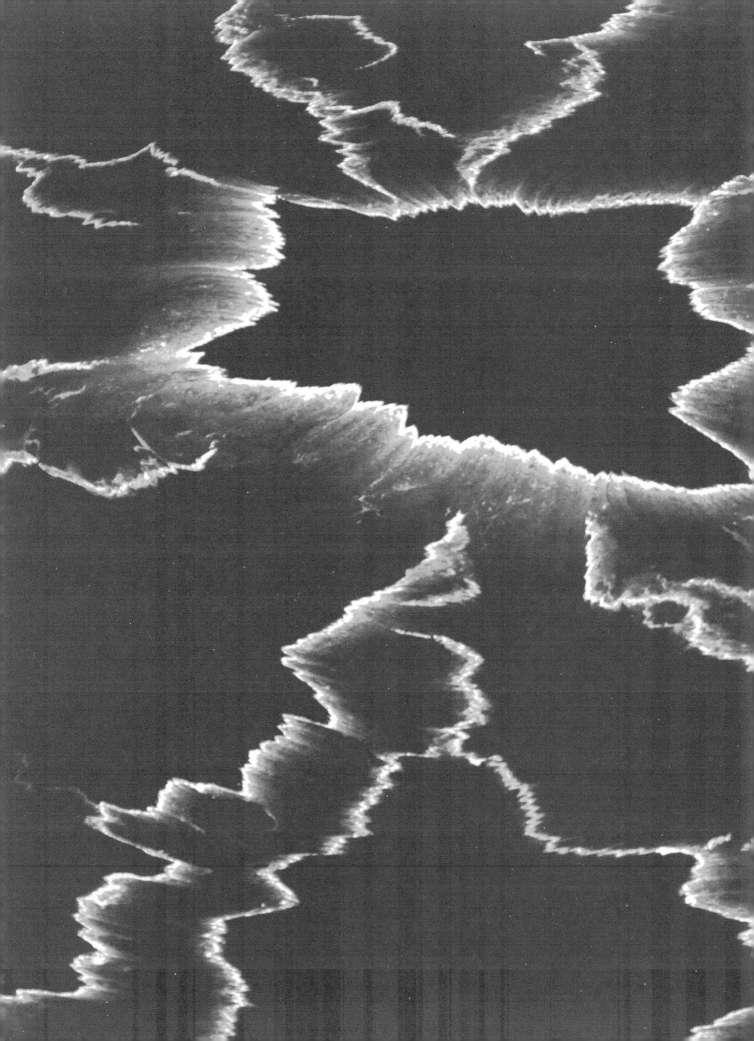